# Miami

Craig & Cheri Howard

Cover Image: Downtown Miami from Rickenbacker Causeway
Back Cover: Sunrise near Black Point Park

Designed and Published: Craig Howard at Fonts & Film
1103 Truman Avenue, Key West, FL
email: craighowardkeywest@yahoo.com

Printed in China

ISBN: 0-9713531-2-3

Freedom Tower - Biscayne Boulevard

Green-backed Heron at Fairchild Tropical Gardens - Coral Gables

South Pointe - Miami Beach

Parrot Jungle Island

Everglades National Park

Calle Ocho - Little Havana

Crandon Park Marina - Key Biscayne

Rickenbacker Marina
Virginia Key

Ancient Spanish Monastery - North Miami Beach

Sunflower - Fruit and Spice Park

Solomon Islands Orchid - Fairchild Tropical Gardens

Bird of Paradise - Fairchild Tropical Gardens

Annato (Lipstick Tree) - Fruit and Spice Park

Water Lily - Fairchild Tropical Gardens

Canna Lili - Everglades Alligator Farm

Miami Jai-Alai

Lincoln Road Mall - Miami Beach

Tequesta Family Monument
Brickell Avenue Drawbridge

Space Shuttle Challenger Memorial
Bayfront Park

South Miami Beach

Miami Seaquarium - Virginia Key

American Airlines Arena - Biscayne Boulevard

Jackie Gleason Theater of the Performing Arts - Miami Beach

Fruit and Spice Park - Homestead

Downtown Miami

South Beach

Hialeah Park and Race Course

Vizcaya Museum and Gardens

Miccosukee Indian Arts Festival

Miami Beach Botanical Garden

Haulover Marina - North Miami Beach

Fisher Island

Miami Seaquarium - Virginia Key

Ocean Drive - Miami Beach

Coral Castle - Homestead

Grand Prix Americas on Biscayne Boulevard

Sunrise over Card Sound Road

Coral Gables City Hall

Miami Metrozoo

Stilt Village - South of Key Biscayne

Port of Miami

Roosters of Little Havana

Biltmore Hotel
Coral Gables

Coral Gables
Congregational Church

ENTERING
CRANDON PARK
MIAMI-DADE COUNTY PARK AND RECREATION DEPT.

CAFETERIA

VILLAGE OF KEY BISCAYNE

Jackie GLEASON
Theater of the Performing Arts

BOX OFFICE HOURS
M - F 10:00 - 5:30
FOR THEATER INFORMATION
CALL 305-673-7300

Sunshine Tropical Foliage
WHOLESALE ONLY

OCEAN PALM

PIER 5

Hialeah Park
CLUBHOUSE ENTRANCE

Delicious
KEY LIME JELLY

Everglades National Park

Gulfstream Park - Hallandale Beach

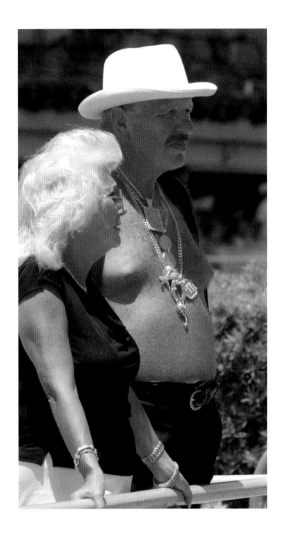

Bill Baggs State Park - Key Biscayne

Sunrise at Newport Fishing Pier

Art Deco District - Miami Beach

Venetian Pools - Coral Gables

Night Falls on Ocean Drive

Key Biscayne Morning

Gulfstream Park - Hallandale Beach

Green Anole
Coral Castle

Bayside Marketplace

Downtown Miami

Holocaust Memorial - Miami Beach

Haulover Marina - North Miami Beach

Everglades Alligator Farm - Homestead

Brickell Avenue

Downtown Miami

Cape Florida Lighthouse - Key Biscayne